THE TUNISIAN TUCK UP

Mainbrace

novum ✈ pro

This book is also available as e-book.

www.novum-publishing.co.uk

© 2016 novum publishing

ISBN 978-3-99048-490-6
Editor: Nicola Ratcliff, BA
Cover photo: Mainbrace
Cover design, layout & typesetting: novum publishing
Illustrations: Mainbrace (3)

www.novum-publishing.co.uk

ACKNOWLEDGEMENT

Firstly, to my dearly loved family who gave every comfort and afforded all the help they possibly could during my detainment, thank you.

Secondly, to the British Army who trained me to survive and evade in almost any situation.

Lastly, but by no means least, to my fallen comrades, who would no doubt have laughed their socks off at my air rifle being confiscated, you are not forgotten, I salute you.

CHAPTER 1

The voyage in

It was still calm in the shelter of the anchorage, but if the weather forecast came true I should have fair winds in a couple of hours. I was well fed and rested, it was late in the afternoon and it made good sense to get the anchor up and go to sea in daylight. I did my last minute checks and went online to check the latest weather update. It was looking good, a nice fresh breeze coming from behind.

I could run down wind using foresail only, perfect when you're single handed. I negotiated the moorings and fish farms in daylight and shortly after that, I was in open water. It was a lovely evening and looked like being a very pleasant trip. It was the 13th of March, approaching the Spring Equinox, which is always a little bit unpredictable weather wise.

I had been monitoring three different weather websites for the last few days and most of their predictions were pretty much spot on, so I was feeling confident. I set the foresail and plotted my course, then watched the sun disappear over the horizon. It was still a bit chilly in the evenings so I went below and put the kettle on.

A few hours passed and we were sailing nicely, jogging along without a care in the world. There was a small island on route and the chart was showing an anchorage outside of the harbour, but protected by the outer sea wall. My plan was to break the journey up into two shorter legs; I could stop and rest up there, before continuing on my way.

I glanced at the instruments and noticed that the boat speed had increased, so I poked my head out of the hatch and the wind strength seemed stronger than before. A quick look at the wind instrument, confirmed that we had six more knots now. The boat was made of steel and quite heavily built. The fact is, she doesn't sail very well in light winds, she needs a blow.

I noticed that the boat was beginning to roll about more; the wind direction had changed slightly and was now on my port quarter. The wave height was increasing as the wind became stronger and the swell was now lumping into me.

It was almost gale force now, but I wasn't too bothered by that, I was a seasoned sailor and the boat was a lot tougher than me.

My school had a canoeing and sailing club, by the time I was ten years old, I was a competent dingy sailor and I've never looked back, its been a passion ever since. I particularly enjoy the challenge of single handed sailing; I was in my element and had been caught out in some seriously bad weather over the years. I decided to go on deck and reduce sail, the boat was going too fast and was sailing off the wave crests, then falling into the troughs, all very uncomfortable. Soon afterwards, the waves were catching me up slowly, picking me up gently and putting me down in a nice easy motion.

Less than an hour later, there were forty three knots of wind and a severe gale, so I had to go up again and furl more sail away. It was nearly dawn and I was closing in quickly on the island. I reached for the pilot book with the port plan in and because the wind direction had changed in the night, it was going to make it difficult to enter the harbour. I calculated the arrival time, I should be somewhere near in about four hours. I was feeling a bit tired and very hungry, there was no way I was going to try and cook in these conditions, so I put my hand in the galley cupboard and found the Marmite. Gripping the jar between finger and thumb, and holding a hand rail with the remaining three fingers, I found a spoon with the other hand.

It wasn't quite as pleasant as a hot drink, but it wasn't going to scold me, I washed it down with a glass of mineral water. As I was putting the jar away, I spotted the marmalade and dug my spoon into that as well, that actually seemed to give me some zest. There was just one boiled (high energy) sweet left, I smiled to myself and put it in my pocket. Now in daylight, I could see everything through the wheelhouse windows, everything was fine and with any luck, I would be in the harbour and asleep on my bunk in a few hours.

Visibility wasn't good, to say the least, but I was expecting to have sight of the island any time now. Shortly afterwards it came into view and I made a slight course change, so as to be a safe distance offshore. I wanted sea room and time to observe the conditions in the entrance. When I arrived, I grabbed the binoculars and braced myself in the hatchway, oh blast, it was horrific.

The waves were crashing up against the breakwater and rebounding to meet the other incoming waves, it was a complete turmoil. To even think about attempting an entry would have been crazy. That meant my original passage plan was completely out of the window, all I could do was sail on by and re-evaluate the situation.

As the island disappeared from view, a sudden squall came through, it read sixty one knots and lasted for about three minutes then dropped down to a steady forty eight to fifty. I went to study my chart; the next problem was, at my present speed, I would be blown onto the Tunisian coast in the hours of darkness. I was just thinking about putting my waterproofs on and furling what little sail was left, when the whole boat shuddered. There was a loud bang followed by the horrible roar of a sail, flogging itself to pieces. I knew if it fouled itself up and I couldn't take it down, there was a real possibility that the boat and I would be lost on some piece of coastline. There was no time for waterproofs, this was very urgent. When I got to the foredeck I saw that the furling line had chafed and parted, the whole sail had released itself.

I cut what frayed line was left on the drum, then reattached what was left and took it directly onto one of the mast winches. I was able to furl it away but it was a bodge and I wanted to make sure it didn't happen again. Where I was standing at the mast, there were some short pieces of line that I kept there for just such emergencies. I grabbed one and carefully made my way back to the bow. I leant against the forestay, so as to free up both hands and reach out to pass the line around it. Just then, a wave hit and I fell backwards. I landed back first on the anchor windlass, the pain was instant and intense. I couldn't move, I was sat on the fore deck soaking wet and cold from the wind chill and hanging on, in near hurricane force winds.

I needed to sort my act out and quickly. The pain was coming from the rib cage but there didn't appear to be any spine damage, but in any case I couldn't stay here I had to get myself back inside somehow. With the wind and salt spraying in my face, I crawled along the side deck with my eyes closed, going from hand hold to hand hold, from memory. I managed to get myself into the hatchway and could open my eyes again. All I had to do now was get down the steps. Once inside, I sat on the floor, in a door frame and braced myself, with my legs. With no sail up and no engine, the boat was crashing about in what were now, seven meter waves, but she could take it. I needed to look at my own problems now.

I put my left hand behind me and applied some pressure on the ribs then braced myself for the pain, I covered my mouth with the other hand and forced a cough, there was no sign of any blood. I wouldn't normally have done that for fear of causing more damage but I wasn't about to get an x-ray and I needed to know how bad things were.

The wind chill on deck had gone through my wet polo shirt and I was very cold. I raised my arms to pull the wet shirt off, the pain made me draw a sharp breath, which also hurt.

I reached in my pocket to find my knife, I'd have to cut it off. Just as I was about to open the knife, another huge wave slammed into the side and I lunged forward. To impale myself on my own knife wouldn't exactly improve my current situation, I decided it was quite a nice shirt; I'd keep it on for a while. As I slipped the knife back into my pocket I felt something small and pulled it out, it was my boiled sweet. I thought I was due a break, I popped the sweet in my mouth and braced in my doorframe I sucked on it until the cherry flavoured delight had completely gone.

From my doorframe I could see all the instruments. I knew it was clear open sea all the way to Tunisia, the only danger was other shipping and I couldn't see out of the windows. I must force myself to get up. Once up, I started the engine and put us back on a course. Straight away, the violent motion eased slightly, and with the engine running, I had all the battery power I needed, I turned the radar on. At our present speed, we would indeed be dangerously close to land well before dawn. I had only enough engine revs on to work the autopilot so as to minimise boat speed. The only other thing was, to put in a few dog legs and zig zag my way to increase the mileage. This meant that the wind and waves were now catching me up as before, and things onboard were a lot more comfortable.

I gently sat back down in the security of my doorframe and now with the radar on, I didn't need to see out of the windows, that thing could see much further than I could, especially in these conditions.

I turned my thoughts to planning ahead and avoiding any potential problems. I wasn't able to attach the safety line on the foresail furler, that was washed overboard by the same wave that injured me. I could only hope the bodge repair held up until we were in port. I certainly wasn't going back out there, unless my life depended on it.

The engine was purring away nicely. In calm weather I've rarely experienced engine problems, any muck and dirt just lays in the bottom of the tanks. It's only when the boat starts rolling about, that it all gets stirred up and clogs the filters, that would be all I needed right now.

Anyway, I had recently serviced my dearly loved Perkins and drained both fuel tanks it should get me to a safe haven somewhere. I had spare filters at hand but was in no physical condition to be climbing around the engine room in this weather and bleeding air out of the system with fan belts and alternators spinning furiously in such a confined space.

I turned my thoughts back to forging some kind of plan and deciding which port to head for. I eased myself up and went to the chart table, the zig zag tactics had worked well and considerably improved things. I was now forty miles offshore and it would be daylight in three hours, so which port then?

The plans I had of the various different ports along the coast and the wind direction, persuaded me to alter my course for Mahdia. The layout of the port was such that, if I put full speed on, there was only about two hundred meters of significant danger and once I had rounded the breakwater, we were home free. That was the new plan then, I could see from the drawing that there wasn't that much room inside and I wasn't going to be able to jump around at the last minute. All the mooring lines and fenders needed to be laid out before I arrived and with any luck, and I felt I was due some, there would be someone on the quayside to help.

I sat back down and watched the instruments; my clothes had nearly dried but were still cold and clammy with the salt. With the engine still purring away as sweet as a nut and the heater on, it was quite comfortable inside. The thought of going on deck to prepare the mooring lines didn't turn me on at all, and anyway if the wind changed direction again, the plan could well change too.

Also, if a mooring line was washed over the side and made fast to the boat at one end, it would trail along side and the next thing would be a fouled propeller. I didn't fancy going for a swim with the bread knife between my teeth, and in this sea state, I would be very lucky to get back onboard. It's more likely that I would die in the water. I would wait for a bit and certainly until daybreak, anyway.

As a dim loom of light appeared on the horizon, to the east, my spirit lifted immensely. I went to the chart table again and double checked everything, as exhausted as I was it would be easy to make a mistake or overlook something. But I hadn't, it was all working out now and it was nearly time to prepare the mooring lines, only this time I would wear my waterproofs.

Putting them on was a painful task but I would have to work carefully and take my time so I expected to be on deck for a while. As I knelt down and reached in the locker the pain was severe, it took everything I had just to lift the ropes out of the locker.

It was daylight now and the wind started to reduce, I had experienced this several times before when a storm would rage all night and then die away to nothing, at daybreak or shortly afterwards. I hoped that would be the case today. Indeed it was, as I worked, it became calmer and easier. The boat had slowed down and there was less spray blowing from the wave crests. The waves were still high, but the boat was riding up and down a lot smoother and hanging on, while I worked. It wasn't anywhere near as painful as before. The lines were soon ready and I returned to the warmth of the wheelhouse. Now that the boat had slowed down, my arrival time would be later, around midday I thought, but that didn't matter, for every hour that past, the waves would slowly reduce. I rounded the breakwater at 11.47 with no trouble at all and was alongside the quay just before midday. The police were ambling about, but didn't offer any help. Thankfully, a couple on another boat just in front of me, took my lines and helped me tie up. As soon as the last mooring line was made fast, I slumped down on the cockpit seat with my elbows on my knees and my head in my hands, the boat was safe. Or I thought it was, little did I know my ordeal was only just beginning.

CHAPTER 2

The Reception

Midday 16th of March.

As I sat there with my head in my hands, I felt myself starting to shut down. I could hear voices but they sounded very distant, when I opened my eyes everything was blurred. I had been running on adrenalin and the supply was subsiding. I could hear, Documents, give Documents, want passport.

I half raised my right hand and said "Okay sure just give me a minute." I had previously laid my documents on the chart table in readiness, I took hold of the rigging and tried to stand up, I couldn't, I slumped back down, and as I did a sharp pain shot up my left side. I let a slight grunt go and then heard laughter. I tried again to get to my feet and this time managed it.

Slowly, I made my way down the steps and picked up my folder, then went on deck again. The police office was right on the quayside, only 5 meters from the boat, thankfully. I went into the office and was told to sit at a table with a police officer opposite. He was talking in French and I didn't understand a word, my second language is Spanish; also I'd forgotten to pick up my glasses. I couldn't read a newspaper headline in this state. He put his elbow on the table and cupped his hand under his chin; he glared at me as though I had offended him, then turned the paper around and started to fill it in on my behalf.

"Wine," he said "wine." I had previously been told by another yachtsman that I'd met the year before, a bottle of wine will get you everywhere. All I wanted to do was get to bed. "Yes wine," I said "you can have wine." He was still speaking French and becoming a little bit annoyed with me, I really was doing my very best. He ticked away at the form, then turned it around and stabbed his finger where he wanted me to sign. I didn't understand what I was signing but all my papers were in order and it was only a port police form and I didn't feel up to making a fuss. He beckoned me to leave, ahh my bed at last.

As hungry as I was, I just wanted to lay my head down, no sooner had I done so, then there was the sound of footsteps and voices, three men clambering about on deck calling "hello hello." I got myself up, the customs had arrived, oh well might as well get it done then I can eat and sleep as much as I liked. They were speaking English, that was easier, "Good afternoon Customs," they said. "Yes please come in" I replied. One was in plain clothes, another was in uniform and wearing body armour, he was carrying a side arm on his belt and the other was a short fat young man with big dirty boots, in a kind of mixed dress. As they entered the wheelhouse they spotted the electronic instruments, these were permanently installed since the boat was new and no different to any other vessel. They said "you must declare" I said yes I have nothing to hide. He asked me for a piece of paper then told me to list all electrical equipment.

Still absolutely exhausted I started the list, there were constant interruptions from the other two officers who were searching the other cabins and my concentration was not at its best anyway. One of them asked "Do you have a camera?" "Well, yes on my mobile." I replied. Then he produced a camcorder from behind his back, "And this" he said "you must declare." That was about six years old and had been left onboard by my ex girlfriend, I had forgotten I had it. Now I was desperately trying to focus on what else was onboard, I had a food blender, a shaver and hair trimmer, then there was a call from the forward cabin, alcohol you have lots of alcohol. Yes I replied, I have lots of everything in preparation for the coming sailing season I have tinned and dried food and cleaning products, tea and coffee and especially alcohol because I didn't think it was on sale here and anyway its not illegal to have alcohol on board.

"You must declare" he said. "Yes well, I'm still trying to declare my bloody electronics, I can't be in three places at once, be reasonable please." Then came a call from the after cabin "What is this?" "One moment please I'm coming." I shouted back. He was referring to the gun cabinet; I went for the keys and unlocked it. Inside were an air rifle and my shotgun and also the license for it, which I handed him while I produced the guns. When they saw them their eyes lit up like children in a toy shop, they were passing them to each other and babbling away in Arabic at the top of their voices. The little fat one lost interest in my alcohol and waddled his way to the after cabin to join the party.

I also had a one inch emergency flare pistol registered on the same certificate but during the storm the night before I had seen fit to remove the previous customs seal on the cabinet door to have it at hand just in case, it was in my draw along with the cartridges. It was the uniformed man who had called me and was now waving the shotgun about trying to open the breach. It was a pump action gun and you had to press a detent button to open it. I held my hand out and he passed it to me. I opened the breach and showed him it was not loaded then eased the firing pin and reapplied the safety catch. In the meantime, fatty had found the flare pistol and figured out how to load it. He put a cartridge in, inside the boat. Before he could close it, I grabbed it with my hand across the hammer and snatched it from him. When I had made it safe, I laid it down and told him to get out.

The search seemed to have paused, I asked why and they told me they were waiting for their boss to arrive, and in due course he did, well two of them actually, both in plain clothes. The uniformed man took the guns into the wheelhouse and squatted down with them across his leg, while one of the newcomers produced a camera and took several photos. He was looking very pleased with himself; you would have thought he had just shot a Bengal Tiger at the very least. I bet this was going to be big news tomorrow. I said "Are you going to put the guns away now and put your seal on the cabinet?" "No we are taking them, but they are legally in my possession and registered in my name, why?" He repeated "We are taking them." I said "Okay, on one previous occasion customs have taken the shotgun into bond and issued me with a receipt to reclaim it immediately before my departure, can I have my receipt please." He reached into his jacket pocket and pulled out a piece of folded paper, he unfolded it and waved it in my face pointing to my signature "You did not declare."

It was the form I had signed earlier; it wasn't the port police form it was a customs declaration form. I was absolutely gutted and knew straight away that I was in trouble. I kicked myself far harder than they could have done; how did I allow myself to fall into a trap like this? I pointed out that the air rifle was not a firearm and required no certification; "We are taking it" he said. I noticed fatty was sitting on the wheelhouse, smoking; he had the sole of his boot on the window and his other foot on a deck fitting. He was applying significant pressure to the glass, enough so that I could see the sole distort from inside. The window was 10mm marine grade toughened glass. The fat little prick would have to eat a lot more pies before he could put a rubber soled boot through that. But it was the shear fact that he was being as disrespectful as he possibly could. Anyway there were more pressing things to get my head round, I ignored him.

I asked one of the more senior men why the search seemed to have paused again, we are waiting for our boss, I was hoping at his level perhaps I could explain how this all came about and appeal to his good nature. No chance, he arrived in a light grey suit. He was a big well fed man, and wearing nearly enough aftershave to disguise his body odour, he had clean shoes at least, but he was a nasty looking piece of work. There were now seven men onboard, they had me over a barrel and they were revelling in it. The chief (grey suit) was emptying my bedside cabinet, which was home to my most prized personal possessions. I stayed with him, watching carefully. I had a very nice dress watch of some considerable value, he held it for a second or two, looked at me then dropped it on my bed. I put it on my wrist, that wasn't going to disappear. Then he pulled out my military medals and some insignia, after looking at them he dropped them on the floor. I gave him what's known in the trade as, the death stare. He picked them up and put them back in the cabinet, and with some care. He found my beret, it was old and light in colour, not looking at its best; he replaced that too. He then turned his attention to my DVD collection, they were all original discs in the plastic case, many of them still with the price on, no pirate copies at all.

As he systematically opened each one with his back to me, I returned to the wheelhouse, where the other Officers, NO I won't call them officers, that would be an insult to all gentleman everywhere. The others were still busy playing with their new toys. I had made my point with grey suit, but obviously wasn't going to get anywhere, they were all now addressing me as Captain, albeit in a smarmy disrespectful manner, but it was an improvement anyway. I had been studying each character carefully and decided to approach one of the senior plain clothes men, "Excuse me sir, may I know your name?" "My name is Smiles," he said. "Well smiles, I would like to apologise for this misunderstanding, I have a bottle of fine Scotch whisky and some traditional ginger wine from London, can I offer you something to compensate you for this inconvenience and maybe we can resolve this problem? He simply said "No." "Well, can we please get on with the search, I've been three days now without food or sleep and I'm injured." I responded. "Don't worry," he said "we will search."

I went back to grey suit, who was sitting on my bed, looking through my photo albums; he looked at me with a blank expression that revealed nothing about his mood or thoughts. Many years ago, I had worked as a convoy leader for Save the Children in the Sudan, taking food aid to starving Muslims. While I was there HRH Princess Anne paid us a visit and I was very privileged to have met her. In the album, there were photos of us together while I showed her Royal Highness one of the trucks. There was another album laid open on the bed, beside him. Many years after that I had worked in Bosnia, during the war, running aid convoys into Sarajevo under fire while the city was under siege. The aid effort saved many lives including the Muslim inhabitants. HRH Prince Charles, flew in to Metkovic by chopper on a surprise visit and I had the great honour of meeting his Royal Highness too, there were photos of this in that album. I smiled at grey suit and said "You really have completely misjudged me, I'm not a bad man I came here as a friend." He stood up and his face returned to its normal aggressive scowl, well that didn't cut any ice then.

But at least they were getting on with the search now; they were completely ransacking the whole boat. Grey suit picked up my clarinet and tried to blow it, he couldn't. He then forcefully pulled it apart with a wringing motion, looked inside and stuffed it back together like a neanderthal thug. He continued searching, emptying my wardrobe and delving into every jacket pocket, my clothes were scattered everywhere. He then upturned the bed, there was storage space below it. I was beginning to feel a bit aggressive myself and becoming more and more angry. Even at my age, in my late fifties, I would have taken great delight in meeting him in a boxing ring or on a karate mat. I decided to just walk away and leave him to it. I would continue to conduct myself as an English gentleman for as long as the situation allowed. Smiles put a cigarette in his mouth, but before he could light it, I said "No not in here, outside." He went on deck and left his ash and cigarette end with all the others that had amassed over the course of this very long day. It was nearly dark now and grey suit emerged from the after cabin, "torch do you have a torch?" he asked. I handed him a torch and he disappeared again. Then he returned and asked for a screwdriver, o bloody hell surely not. I reluctantly found him a screwdriver and he set about removing some of the interior panels. They continued trashing my boat until after half past ten, then eventually picked up my guns and left. As they were leaving, I was told they would return in the morning to take me to their Headquarters. As they left I looked around the boat, it was a disaster area but I couldn't face tackling the clean up tonight, and anyway there could be more of the same tomorrow. Just then, there was a gentle tap on the side of the boat, it was the couple from the other boat who had kindly helped me tie up when I arrived. "Are you okay? they said. "Well no not really I'm in a bit of a mess." "We were going to invite you to dinner, we've saved you some would you like to come over?" they asked. I think if my ribs weren't so painful I would have hugged them both to death. I enjoyed a wonderful meal, I said I was very tired and excused myself. They bid me goodnight and said they would see me tomorrow. I replied "I truly hope so, but they are returning in the morning to take me away." And they did.

CHAPTER 3

The False Charges

Having dined well in good company I made my way back on-board. As I entered the wheelhouse and saw the mess, my morale dropped again, there was nowhere to lay down or even sit for that matter. Every bunk or seat cushion was totally upheaved. I went into the after cabin, my mattress was on the floor and half curved up the side of the bed. Apart from the boot marks, it looked very inviting. That would have to do for tonight I laid myself down and pulled some of my scattered clothes over me; in no time at all I was asleep.

At 6:30 am, I was awakened by a passing fishing boat. As I opened my eyes and saw the mess, my thoughts returned to yesterday and left me wondering what would unfold today. I was partly rested but could have slept for the rest of the day. If only I could, but I knew the mob were coming for me and there was no way I would get back to sleep now.

My face felt like a cheese grater and I was gasping for a nice cup of tea. I shaved while waiting for the kettle, then searched through the mess to find something to wear today. I was now just waiting and decided to rebuild the wheelhouse seat and re-stow the equipment that normally lives under it. At least I had a seat again; I made another cup of tea and enjoyed it in comfort. I should really eat something, as there was no telling when my next chance would be.

There were tins of food all over the place in the galley, something cold and quick would do for now. Yes perfect, I found a tin of corned beef and some baked beans. I ate my breakfast and made my way to the shower in the after cabin. There was a first aid kit and medical supplies in the cabinet, well there used to be. I was looking for pain killers; shortly, I spotted them, took one and put the rest in my pocket. I suddenly realized that I smelt nearly as bad as gray suit. The shower tray was heaped with all kinds of things. Anyway, I needed to replace a panel before it was usable, I put some aftershave on. They hadn't stipulated a time so I couldn't go and find a shop. Some fresh bread and milk would have been nice. I could see a bank through the binoculars, and hoped there was an ATM because as yet, I had no Dinar.

If they arrived and I wasn't here, it was quite likely going to irritate them and I was keen to start the day in the best possible way. I was hoping to contact my family. There was no sim card in my iPhone but just in case I could get Wi-Fi I took it with me. There was a low battery warning, to be expected I suppose, it hadn't been charged for three days. Now where on earth do I start looking for the charging lead? I didn't get a chance, the dirty boots had arrived, "Good morning Captain." "Yes good morning to you." I said and locked the boat. There were three of them, one I hadn't seen before, Smiles and the other guy, that had arrived with him yesterday.

He was everyone's best friend, yesterday he kept saying to me "Don't worry, it's okay." I think he was trying to play the role of good cop and gain my trust. I didn't trust any of them, any further than I could spit against a hurricane. I nicknamed him Slithering Sid. As we walked the short distance to the car, neither of them produced handcuffs, so far so good. Yesterday Grey Suit had seen my old fighting knife in the bedside cabinet, along with my other keepsakes. He hadn't batted an eyelid at it, but they knew I had it. The new one opened the rear door and asked me, quite politely, to get in without asking me to empty my pockets or search me at all. I was starting to assess their level of professionalism. Smiles drove off with Sid beside him and the new one with me in the back, it was only a short drive to the office and I sat there quietly.

When we arrived, I was escorted up a flight of stairs and into quite a large office. I was given a chair in front of a heavy wooden desk that I would have been proud of. Very different from the

Formica table in the Police station. They sat me down and it all began, "So Captain, you know you must declare. It's the same in all the world, you did not declare." I said I had arrived in an exhausted state, both physically and mentally, with injuries and there were problems with the language barrier, "I haven't deliberately tried to hide anything from you I wasn't given a reasonable chance." I told them.

"But non declaration is non declaration, it is against the law." The fact that I was here made it plainly obvious that they were going to stitch me up. I was trying to create a silly tourist image in the hope that they would slap my hand and send me on my way.

Ever since they laid their eyes on those guns, they were intent on taking them. I thought they might settle for that. There were several men in the office now, including the uniformed man who'd found the gun cabinet, while I was declaring my electronics yesterday. He was sneering at me and looked very smug.

Coffees were brought in and passed around, I wasn't offered one, not that I wanted it. "So Captain, why do you have a shotgun on your boat? I have a clay pigeon trap; it's a sport of mine." I said confidently. "Your colleagues can verify that they saw it onboard yesterday? And the rifle?" "It's an air rifle, we all seem to be forgetting that. But in answer to your question, it's for target shooting, they saw the targets too." I responded, slightly frustrated. He said something to Smiles in Arabic and Smiles nodded his head; there was a pause, while he seemed to be getting his thoughts together. I decided to take the initiative, "Look, regarding the air rifle, it requires no certification in your country, or mine and so requires no special declaration, no more than a dinner plate or a pair of shoes. It was taken from me illegally, return it please." "That won't be possible," he said "they have both been sent to an expert for valuation." "May I ask why?" I questioned. "Yes," he said "you will be fined the current market value in Tunisia and the guns will be destroyed." Yeah like I believe that, his buddies were probably out playing again, just as they had been yesterday, I hope they shoot each other, and judging by their weapon handling skills I witnessed the day before, there was a good chance of it. I replied "Isn't it enough that you have taken a legal gun, now you want to keep it and make me pay for it?" "Not keep it, it will be destroyed." "Well I'm very fond of it, I would very much like to have the pieces back when you've finished." That didn't exactly go down well but he knew I was suspicious.

He sat at his desk and began typing, the room had gone quiet now, so I patiently sat there. As he prepared my charge sheet, I was wondering how they would respond to a medical emergency, it would be a bit awkward for them if I fell off my perch in their office, there would be a mountain of embarrassing paperwork. If I was taken to hospital, I may even get an x-ray and that could only help my case. I took the painkillers from my pocket and with my right hand on my chest, covering my heart, I held them up, "Can I have some water please? I feel very ill." Their heads raised from the keyboard, they crowded round, looked at me, and one of them pointed to the coffee glasses on a small table. "In the toilet" he said. "Err okay, well thanks for your concern!" I needed to take a pee anyway. I was never any good at theatricals, so I returned to my chair. It seems they all have their own little coffee glass, and the owner said "Have you washed it?" "Yes," I replied and I had, but not in the hand basin.

The document was finished at last and the printer went into orbit, it was spitting out page after page. This unnerved me a bit, it was a lot of paperwork.

The glasses were cleared and the table was moved directly in front of where I was seated, then the papers were laid out on the table. Every page was in Arabic. I said "Look guys, the reason I'm here now is because, yesterday I stupidly signed a form that I didn't understand. I am sorry but I can't sign these, I need translations in English." I was reminded that they did have the powers of arrest, I couldn't afford to let that happen, if they jailed me, the boat would be stripped out or go missing completely! I sat quietly. One of them picked the phone up and called someone. After the call he said "Okay, ten minutes."

About half an hour later, a man arrived and introduced himself as my translator. He pulled a chair up beside me and said, "I will read it to you." "I would rather read it myself in my own language" I said. He picked up a page and read it to himself, then he said "This is a very minor infraction of the law." "Well then, why so many documents?" I asked. "There are seven copies of a three page document" he said and I could see that they were laid out in threes. I asked what the charge was and he told me it was non declaration and very minor. I said "In my country it was serious enough, what are the consequences?" "You will be fined." he replied. "How much?" I asked. "Maybe 300 Dinars." Oh well, right or wrong that's not the end of the world and if it finishes this mess, I'll go along with that. A fingerprint pad was put on the table and my print was put on all seven copies, beside where I would sign. No sooner was it done and I was told I could leave. The translator needed 100 Dinar for his services and so he took me to a bank and then dropped me off near the boat.

I was back onboard by 3:30 and was feeling a bit more at ease. After all, 300 Dinar is only just over £100. I wasn't happy about being ripped off but I wanted this resolved. I got myself a beer from the fridge and sat in the wheelhouse, on the seat I had replaced that morning. Looking at my red fingers, I felt like a criminal. Well what have they actually got on me. The air rifle is legal, the shotgun was legally in my possession and has been registered in my name with the same constabulary for twenty five years, and during all that time I haven't had so much as a parking ticket. The license had expired some time before, but I had emailed the Firearms officer and printed out the reply which was clipped to the certificate.

I was told it wasn't possible to renew the licence until I returned to the UK and was available for interview. When I did return, I would hand the gun in and submit my renewal application. So they were happy for me to continue keeping it onboard and there was no time stipulation. No offence committed. I had made no false declarations. It all boiled down to a piece of paper in a foreign language, filled in by somebody else amounting to non declaration and even that was due to extenuating circumstances. I should have a little faith in the translator and stop worrying.

I didn't want to sleep on the floor again tonight so I set about putting my cabin back in some kind of order, it was a mess. I put everything back under the bed in its usual place and made the bed then started clearing the floor. One of the DVD cases was open, the disc was missing, then another, I placed the cases to one side expecting to find the discs amongst the rest of the confusion. When I had re-hung my clothes, there was little left on the floor and no discs. I suspected they were in the pocket of a Grey Jacket. I picked my clarinet up and inspected it, wondering how it had coped with the rough handling. The cork joints were badly damaged, the scum had broken my clarinet.

I decided to go for a gentle stroll and get a pizza from near where the translator had dropped me earlier and then get an early night. Tomorrow I would start work in the galley and then I was able to cook again.

That didn't happen; I had only been up a short while and was drinking my normal morning tea when the mob arrived again. What the hell do they want now, the spear fishing gun or my catapult? I poked my head out of the hatch and said "Yes what is it? "You must come with us" they said. What for now, I wondered. I wasn't ready, I told them I needed to use the toilet and finish dressing. "You have fifteen minutes, be ready." As I was dressing, an amusing thought came to me, I could take the empty DVD cases and say to Grey Suit, "Here please take them, I have no further use for them." But to provoke him without good reason was not a good idea. If anyone was going to jail me, that arsehole would.

Shortly before 8:30 am, we were getting into the car. As we arrived, the translator was already there and waiting. After the good mornings I said "What's this all about?" "There is another document," he said "but don't worry I will translate everything." We went upstairs to the same office, Sid was busy bidding all his friends good morning and as I entered, he ushered me to the same chair that I had sat in the day before. I had a horrible suspicion that I was being shafted again and wasn't at all convinced that the translator was working for me at all, he knew every one of them by name and they were talking away like old friends. As I sat there wondering what colour my fingers would be today they suddenly changed back to English.

The translator told me that the valuation had been confirmed and we could now complete the final document. "That was quick and efficient," I said "and what is the value?" "2800 Dinar" he said. That sounded rather high so I asked how they had arrived at that conclusion. "Well the air rifle has a high price and the market value has to include the customs import duty." "And my shotgun?" "Yes," he said "the same applies." "So what now?" I asked. "You are required to pay a fine of the equivalent amount." "But yesterday you told me the fine would be around 300 Dinars and I signed on the strength of that." "Yesterday we didn't know the value" he said, "but don't worry we can negotiate." It was plainly obvious that they were going to throw the book at me and extort as much money out of me as they possibly could. I wasn't about to give them any reason to jail me and I had already signed myself into trouble. If it went to court I had signed in the presence of a translator and my appraisal of things was that any honourable Judge would hear my case and see the original form that I had signed on my arrival. Surely it would be kicked out of Court.

I told the translator that I didn't have that much money, "Don't worry we can negotiate" he said, again. Then he said something in Arabic and it all turned very frosty. I was alone in a room with six of them on their territory and with no witnesses. I was hoping this wasn't going to turn into a back room job; my ribs weren't really up to taking a good kicking.

Many years before, I had trained and served with the very best, the interrogation and phychology training was flashing back to me, I began to use it. I adopted the Grey man stance. A technique used by special forces while under interrorgation. It wasn't very long before they started again, "So Captain you bring illegal firearms into Tunisia, you have caused us a lot of trouble and concern. Of course you will be fined."

From what I could see, they were loving it, not making eye contact with any of them I simply said "I'm sorry." "Why were the weapons hidden?" "They were correctly and responsibly secured in an approved gun cabinet that had been inspected by the firearms officer, when I was granted permission to carry them onboard. They were not hidden." I replied. "But you did not declare," "I have explained the circumstances of my arrival many times. Then Smiles said "Yes you were tired."

Then I was asked the value of my boat, I didn't like the sound of that at all, why would they ask that unless they were going to snatch the boat. I knew the rough value of it but decided to under state it. My first answer was, well its ten years old and is in need of a repaint and some other superficial work, I really don't know. I wasn't going to mention any defects that would allow them to enforce the repairs, before I was allowed to leave, if I was allowed to leave at all. "Just a rough value, you must have some idea." he said. "Well it would need to be surveyed," I said "but I think maybe €100,000." Now I was a very worried man, what were these despicable bastards up to next?

Shortly after that, the printer burst into life and began spitting out more documents, they were laid out on the table in front of me, as before. The fingerprint pad was placed on the table but had dried out over night; one of them picked it up and kindly spat on it a few times for me. Before I signed the first copy, I wrote under duress above where I should sign. "What is this?" they said and the translator said something in Arabic. The page was snatched away and filed in the rubbish bin; they printed another one off and placed it on the table. I had put the pen down and was sitting with my arms folded, someone moved round behind me and I braced myself but the blow I was expecting wasn't delivered. The man behind the desk opened one of the draws, he put his hand inside and disturbed something that sounded very much like a chain. It must be handcuffs I thought. As I picked the pen up he gently slid the draw closed, I began signing my life away again.

As soon as all the documents were signed, the mood lightened up tremendously. I was told I could leave and the translator offered me a lift, his car was parked 50 meters away on the opposite side of the road. As we were getting into the car, he said "This is my house." "That's convenient, I would imagine you get quite a lot of business from these guys." "Yes," he said "I do." It's a good job he didn't know what I was thinking just at that moment. We drove off and he was being very friendly. "If you need anything you can call me" he said. "Well actually there is something you could help me with, I haven't been able to acquire a Tunisian sim card yet." He drove a bit further and stopped.

"This is a mobile phone shop" he said, pointing across the road. That was handy and I had a translator too, at least he was of some use at last. He dropped me off in the same place and we said our goodbyes, I was pleased to be back on the internet with my iPhone, I could contact my family now. It was about mid afternoon when I unlocked the hatch; I made a cup of tea and set about trying to email my brother. I told him about my problems here and asked him not to panic the rest of the family, especially our father.

Dad was in his eighties and nearly blind. After the Second World War he had served with the Independent Parachute Brigade, during the Suez conflict. He was still very much the British Bulldog and a fine man. I'm immensely proud of him, but he didn't need to be worrying about this at his age. If I was going to cook later, the galley needed a bit of straightening out. I began to pick things up and put them away, it was soon looking a lot better, my floating home was steadily returning to some kind of normality. But I couldn't help wondering how much longer it would be mine.

CHAPTER 4

In Court

Before bedtime we were starting to look ship shape again, I slept well and woke early the next morning. This was now the 19th of March. I was feeling completely rested now but very concerned about the charges against me and had no idea at all how all this would end. An hour or so later, around 9:30 am I was on deck refastening the sail covers that had been undone during the search. Just then the translator appeared round the corner of the office, accompanied by Sid.

"We have some bad news for you," they said "you must appear in court at 8:30 am on the 30th of March" and handed me a document in Arabic. I began opening my mouth to quiz them and decided to say nothing. Sid handed me my Passport and said "You must not leave Mahdia." I asked if he had my boat registration document and firearm certificate, "No" he said they are being retained. After they had left the gravity of the whole situation hit me like a train. I was basically under open arrest and the boat was impounded. It was time to divert my attention away from tidying the boat and concentrate on trying to keep it. Until yesterday I was led to believe that I would have to pay a fine of around 300 Dinars and was prepared to accept that, then yesterday it escalated into the thousands and this morning I receive a summons.

It was painfully obvious that I wasn't going to resolve this on my own, and certainly time to inform the British Embassy of my situation. They quickly responded with very useful lists of English speaking lawyers and translators. There were none locally or anywhere near Mahdia. With the lists there was a form to return giving feedback about satisfaction and value for money along with other relevant questions. That's no doubt why my translator wasn't listed. Next I needed a good lawyer, there was one on the list practicing maritime law but he had no email address and he wasn't answering his phone. Eventually I decided on a firm in Tunis, some 200 km to the north. The initial phone call inspired me with confidence, he was professional and his English was good. He called me soon after, stating his costs, everything included 2000 Dinars and payable in advance by bank transfer.

I contacted my brother; he was a very experienced manager and had worked for a well known UK company for some thirty years. He ran my affairs at home better than I could have done myself and was always helping me out in some way or other. He really is my best friend in the world and never asked for anything in return, except a holiday on the boat occasionally, and that was my pleasure to spend some time with him. There were security measures in place with my bank and not having a UK phone number they contacted my brother to confirm the authenticity of the transfer so I was unable to do it myself from here. He jumped into action and started bailing me out of trouble as usual. The transfer wasn't exactly straight forward due to the request being made in Arabic but he pulled out all the stops and made it happen.

Now I had a lawyer. In due course, he called me to say we needed to meet and he would drive down the following afternoon, when he had finished in court. I didn't see him arrive. I heard voices outside and looked out through the wheelhouse windows. He was in discussion with the police, and they were denying him permission to come on board my boat. I quickly went to meet him and we decided to meet in a restaurant just outside the port, "I'll deal with them tomorrow" he said.

Good lad I thought, he certainly looked the part. As we sat down, a waiter approached the table and he ordered a beer, I gasped in amazement, the mob had given me a right hard time for having alcohol onboard and just four hundred metres from the boat, it was freely on sale. "And for you?" he said. "I'll have the same thank you." Of course this was on me. As we waited for our meal I began to tell him the whole story, he had previously made a reservation in a very nice hotel nearby and was now on Facebook trying to arrange some female company for later in the evening. "I'm sorry," I said "am I interrupting you?" He put his iPad away just as the meal was served.

Having gained his attention the conversation was sounding very positive, especially the issue with the air rifle. "We will claim it back tomorrow" he said and that will reduce the fine. If he achieved just that, he was well on the way to earning his money. The next morning he called to say that his new lady friend had told him it was market day, the road was closed and he couldn't drive in to pick me up. He obviously was in no hurry to tear himself away. I said "I can see the road from here and the traffic seems to be moving ok." He agreed to meet me in one hour. Nearly two hours later he arrived, looking as though he needed to go back to bed.

Anyway it all began, we needed to round up all the paperwork and establish our exact position. I had already given him what little I had and he wanted to talk with the translator. I gave directions to his office and we met him, the lawyer said something and the translator looked very uncomfortable but didn't answer. The Lawyer repeated himself louder this time and stabbed his finger on a document, then the translator reluctantly produced an answer. As we returned to the car I quizzed the Lawyer. It turned out, the document contained serious charges and one of them was brandishing a fire arm at the customs during the search. This was probably when Fatty loaded the emergency flare pistol. I had snatched it and made it safe or when they couldn't figure out how to open the shotgun and I held my hand out and did it for them. But anyway, the translator had just admitted to the lawyer that he had not translated the document to me fully or correctly.

The next stop was the court, we collected what papers were there and sat in the car while he studied them, he did seem to know what he was doing. He explained that there were two separate cases, one was with customs and the other with the courts, and then he told me he would need additional fees, "How much?" I asked. "Not much, just a little" he said. But I needed his services and the ball was rolling now. We made our way to the customs office and climbed the now familiar flight of stairs; he stated his case regarding the air rifle and asked for its return. They simply said no, he tried to argue the point but got nowhere at all, then they all seemed to be ignoring us. As we went back to the car, he looked totally bewildered. "Well," I said, "they won't return it, but it's the law you told me so." "Customs are different" he said, "it's another law."

That had just confirmed what I had already suspected, they were a law unto themselves, and had certainly sent him away with his tail between his legs. In the car I asked him, how serious this was and what was the worst case scenario. He produced a book and found the relevant page. He told me there were three charges, each one had a maximum fine of 2000 Dinars. "Wow!! That's a lot." "Yes" he said "but it could be a jail sentence, it depends on the Judge." I really didn't need to hear that, and my boat. "I haven't seen any paperwork" he said but I don't know.

As he dropped me off outside the port, we arranged to meet outside the court at 7:45 on the morning of the 30th and said our goodbyes. I ambled back to the boat with very little spirit in me at all; it had been a long time since I felt quite as depressed as this. The thought of losing my boat was horrific. I had purchased a set of plans and built it in the UK from scratch, it was my biggest asset, and my home. In the future, when my sailing days were over I had planned to sell it and buy a modest retirement home, this could drastically change my entire life.

I remembered sitting on my father's knee, as a young child and he said to me, "Son, no matter how bad things get you can always look around you and see someone worse off than yourself." He was right wasn't he? I turned my thoughts to all the poor people who had been for a scan and were nervously waiting to hear if they would live or die, and others who were confined to a wheelchair or even a bed for that matter. I needed to put things into perspective. A bit later on, I had a call from the translator, he invited me to join him and his friends in a cafe that evening. They were going to drink coffee and smoke a Hubble bubble pipe. I wasn't feeling particularly friendly towards him but the chance of finding more pieces of information appealed to me and anyway it was better not to burn my bridges.

He picked me up at 7:30. When we arrived, we joined two of his friends at a table in a lounge area and he introduced us. Even before the coffee arrived he started to ask subtle questions about how my day had gone. I told him the lawyer had taken all the paper work and would call me when he had read through everything. I tried in vain to extract anything I could from him but got no further than he had with me. He was obviously a bit concerned about his admission to the lawyer earlier that could only go heavily in my favour and was awkward for him to say the least. It was getting late and he offered to drop me off.

When I got back to the boat I wasn't feeling tired at all, my mind was racing away, I poured a glass of wine and sat outside. A smile came to my face as I wondered how Lawrence of Arabia must have felt all those years ago. As for me, well I was the up and coming Wally of Tunisia. I sat there drinking my wine and trying to make sense of all this. Tourism is their second biggest income; news gets out, were they mad. On reflection that's probably why I wasn't already in detention. I knew of some worldwide sailing websites and forums. Tomorrow I would contact one and see if they were interested in my story. That may put some pressure on and open their eyes to the publicity that would emerge later. But was that wise? Should I wait a few days? The Judge could throw it out and I would have stirred up a Hornet's nest. I poured another glass, and then another. I spent a while just enjoying the cool night air and listening to the crickets, then returned the bottle to the fridge and went to bed.

I awoke with a slightly dull head, but last night's chill out had done me some good. Soon afterwards two European boats arrived and tied up in front of me, where the people that had helped me when I arrived, had previously been. The two boats were cruising together and as I helped to take their lines on the quay, we began to talk. During their four day stay, we socialised and exchanged stories of our sailing adventures. It was nice to have some pleasant company again. After they had left, the days seemed very long and lonely. I was spending far too much time alone on the boat, just waiting to be hauled into court. I couldn't leave Mahdia but I could explore the town while I was here. I ticked the days off and as judgment day neared, I was considering how I should present myself to the court. I decided to wear my Harris Tweed. At the end of March it was beginning to get a bit warm for that kind of attire, here in Tunisia, but that didn't matter. I would meet the Judge looking like an English country gentleman, who would shoot and of course would own a shotgun. The night before, I prepared my clothes and set the alarm for an early start.

I woke before the alarm went off; there was ample time for a good breakfast and some last minute preening. I checked myself over in the mirror and locked the boat. It was still early, I walked the 2 km to the court building and still arrived well before the prearranged meeting time. The sun was up now and the tweed was doing its job. I found some shade and sat waiting for the lawyer. He arrived late again and made a complete fool of himself trying to park his car, when done he said good morning and asked me to get in. He told me he had discovered a law whereby one was allowed eight days to declare firearms in Tunisia and that I had been denied that right, we would proceed on those grounds. I was thinking, so a visitor could spend a week running around armed to the teeth causing complete havoc and leave without making a declaration at all, and I'm facing all sorts of charges for doing nothing wrong, what a crazy place this is.

He straightened his tie in the mirror and put his lawyers cloak on.

As we climbed the steps in front of the court, he actually managed to defy gravity and fall uphill. I said under my breath, "For heaven's sake please don't do that inside." I picked up his brief case and handed it to him. As we entered a large entrance hall I could see what appeared to be chambers and offices bordering the hall. It was very busy, there were people everywhere all babbling away, it was very noisy and quite disrespectful I thought for a court house. The lawyer said he was hoping to speak to the Judge in his chamber before the hearing and disappeared down a corridor. He returned shortly afterwards, looking for his brief case, I had picked it up for safe keeping and handed it to him. He pointed to a door and said "That's the court, you will enter through that door." "Wait here" he said and went about his business again. I managed to find a seat and waited. It seemed like an age when he eventually appeared again. I checked and yes he still had his brief case.

People were starting to enter the court room in their dozens; we shuffled our way in with the rest of them. It was more like a cinema than a court, rows of seats filled with inedited people waiting to be called to the bench. The stack of files on the bench was mountainous, I could be here all day I thought and resigned myself to that fact. It all began, the Judge systematically picked up one file at a time and called the rascal forward. He was very stern and hustled them along. But then he would have to, if he stood any chance of reducing that heap of files. As people walked away with their heads hung low and looking almost suicidal, I began to feel very nervous. The lawyer was talking to a lady who was also wearing a cloak; this is your sworn interpreter he said. A few more cases were heard and then the lawyer said "It's you, it's your turn."

I made my way to the bench without delay, not wanting to waste the courts time. The Judge was now speaking calmly and politely, the lawyer began putting the case to the bench. He was talking for several minutes and totally engrossed in his work, the Judge listened carefully. Afterwards he asked me, "How long have you owned the shotgun?" I turned to the interpreter and she repeated it. "Twenty five years" I replied. Then he asked "Why did you not declare the shotgun?" I told him the circumstances of my arrival and that the form I had thought was a port police form was in French and I hadn't filled it in anyway, but yes I did sign it." He made some notes, then said something to the clerk who was scribbling away at top speed. I was told I could leave and was very happy to do so.

I thanked the interpreter and we made our way back to the car. True to form the lawyer reached the bottom step well ahead of me, I salvaged his brief case again and we went to the car for a chat. He seemed to think it went off okay. He had listened as the Judge repeated things to the clerk and he commented that the Judge was very respectful towards me. "So what now?" I asked. "Well he hasn't jailed you, I'll call you as soon as I know something." "What did he say about the translator's failings in the Customs office? I asked; I didn't mention that, it wasn't necessary. As he began his journey back to Tunis I went back to my shaded spot, it was very warm now and I decided to take a Taxi home. On the way I thought well of course it's necessary, the Judge wasn't there to witness anything, he is assessing the black and white stuff on the bench in front of him. For all his little faults, the lad was doing his best and anyway he had already been paid, it was a bit late to be changing lawyers now and at least his English was good. Back onboard I quickly removed my tweed insulation and opened some hatches. I fancied a nice cup of tea but it was too hot for that, so I sat down with a cold beer. Well that's over with then, all I can do now is wait to hear something.

CHAPTER 5

The wait

I knew, that by the time the lawyer reached his office in Tunis, it would be getting late. There was very little chance of any news today; I may as well busy myself with something constructive.

I had thought about sneaking the boat out in the night, but the security measures here would make that almost impossible and she wasn't ready for sea anyway. I decided I should get her ready though, in case there was an opportunity to make a run for it. I made a list of little things that needed my attention. In the morning, I would start work. First on the list was the oil level in the hydraulic steering system. The next morning I ticked that off the list. Just after I had cleaned up, the phone rang. The lawyer told me that the judgment would be announced on the 14th of April so we had to wait.

I had already been here sixteen days and the thought of spending another two weeks on this concrete wall was not funny. I noticed he Police were being particularly standoffish today; they looked almost indignant and seemed angry that I had not been detained. I had previously noticed that news travels fast here. Everyone seemed to know my situation. I glanced at my list and found the distilled water and after checking the batteries, I ticked that off as well. By the end of the day, she was ready to put to sea, if the chance arose. My normal maintenance, such as rust stains and cleaning, I put on hold. The worse the boat looked at the moment the lower the potential value and anyway, if they did snatch it, I wasn't about to hand it over in pristine condition.

The next thing on my mind was security; there were things on deck that didn't need to be there. I rounded everything up and stowed it safely away, people had been hanging around and looking over the boat, as though I was hosting a car boot sale.

It particularly concerned me when some of the same faces appeared after dark. I was directly in front of the police station but that didn't reassure me at all. To date, the robbers I had encountered were all supposedly official people. My dingy was on davits astern with the outboard motor on and old as it was, the cost of replacing it would have been in the thousands. I would only need to leave the boat unattended for an hour, just at the wrong time and that could disappear. One thing I had was time on my hands; I serviced the outboard and put it away out of sight. I had a cradle on deck, especially made for my little RIB (ridged inflatable boat). I set up my block and tackle and lifted it into place, now it would be very difficult to steal. I had to leave the boat at times for shopping and phone top ups but I deliberately did this randomly, with no routine at all. Sometimes I would walk a few steps down the side of the building, where there were no windows and return again under the pretence that I had forgotten something.

The boat was now as secure as I could possibly make it and I decided to try and relax for a while. The next day a boat arrived and for their two day stay, I had some company again. After I had waved them goodbye and watched their mast top disappear over the harbour wall, I was feeling very bored. Well I needed a hair cut, I could do that. Having found the hair trimmer, I tidied myself up. That took all of fifteen minutes and then I found myself climbing the walls again, this lot were starting to grind me down a bit. It was now the 6th of April and there was over a week left till judgment day. I decided to channel my efforts into making myself as comfortable as possible. I suddenly remembered that my sun shade had been damaged by strong winds, at the end of last summer; it was warming up quickly here and it was in need of repair, before I could use it. Also, it would provide me with some privacy from the police balcony, from which I was constantly being watched.

I found my sail makers' needles and laid the poor thing out on the wheelhouse floor. It was in a right mess, that should keep me occupied I thought. I finished hand sewing for the day and it looked as though it would take another two days to finish it, at least. After breakfast, the next day, I went back to my canvas repairs. Soon after, I heard my name being called, surely not, I must be mistaken then I heard it again and peered out.

It was another single handed yachtsman that I had met twice before in other parts of the Mediterranean. "Hello Jack, what brings you to the middle of nowhere?" I asked him. "I usually come once a year to fill my fuel tanks, it's very cheap" he told me. We were soon sat on my afterdeck sharing a cold beer and chatting away. "So what are your plans for this year?" I asked. "I'm heading east," he said "thought I might spend some time around the Greek islands, and you?" "Well, if I ever get my boat out of here, I'm planning to do the same." I said, sounding slightly frustrated. "What do you mean?" he said. I began to tell him my story, he sat listening with a look of amazement on his face. When I had finished he delved in his pocket and waved his keyring in front of me. It was a miniature pair of handcuffs that actually undone and would clip onto a belt.

I told him his next beer was a warm one, we laughed and continued chatting. He always had been a blagger, but he was good company and if ever I needed it, it was now. "I'm going shopping," he said "can I get you anything?" "Some fresh bread would be nice thank you." As he turned to walk away, I said, "Oh and bring me the till, I've got some heavy fines to pay." He smiled and went on his way. While Jack was here, I decided to put the sunshade on hold and rolled it up.

Over dinner that evening, he said "They want to charge me for mooring on the wall." Well I'm paying," I said "isn't that normal?" "It always used to be free," he said "I mean look there's nothing here, it's a smelly fish dock, no facilities at all." He asked if I would like coffee, I jumped at the chance, he was well known for his excellent coffee and carried a selection of liqueur type flavourings. I chose almond, as usual. Jack stayed until the morning of the 11th and did my morale the power of good. As I helped him cast his mooring lines off, he looked at me with a serious

face and said "It's going to be alright, I will see you In Greece."
"I hope so." I said and wished him a safe journey. I watched him
leave then went below.

By the end of the day, the sunshade was looking a lot better, a
little more work tomorrow and I could put it up. After a rest-
less night I got dressed and put the kettle on. As I was finishing
my tea, I heard some powerful engines, when I looked out I was
absolutely horrified. It was a Customs launch and it was berthing stern right on my bow. This was two days before the judgment was due. What's all this about, I thought, are they preparing to tow my boat away. Their mooring lines were the biggest
frayed and rotten mess I had seen in a long time. They were looking very concerned about one line in particular, that was almost
chafed through.

There were eight men on the launch, including Smiles, and
guess what, Sid was almost a metre away from him, as usual. After a few minutes of shoulder shrugging and arm waving, Sid
started walking towards my boat, with a face like a puppy. I went
on deck to meet him and had already guessed what he wanted;
we have no new ones he said. I wasn't about to give them one
of mine, but I did see an opportunity to do some serious gloat-
ing. Just as he had kept saying to me, when he was playing the
role of good cop "don't worry" I said, the same and paused. He
pointed to the line, I repeated myself, "don't worry." He was
at a complete loss; I pointed to a splice on one of my lines and
said "I will help you." I went below and found my splicing fid
grabbed a roll of tape and my knife and went over to the launch.
"Good morning Smiles," I said "I believe you have a problem
that I can help with."

He looked quite friendly now; I sat myself down and examined
the rope. To do a good repair, I had to cut out four metres of
rot. As I started work, they all gathered round, watching intent-
ly, one young lad especially so. Sid introduced him as the chief
engineer. He was very young for the position he held and never

took his eyes off what I was doing; the boy wanted to learn and had done me no wrong. When the splice was half made, I beckoned him to sit at my side and handed him my Swedish fid, he finished the job under my supervision. I suddenly realised, the police were gathered around too. As we finished, a happy young man shook my hand and he was wearing a very proud smile. I got to my feet and said to Smiles "Are there any more?" "No, not today" he said. As I turned to walk away he said "I'm sorry." I looked him in the eye and nodded my head. I didn't believe for a minute that he was sincere. As I boarded my boat again, I felt I had turned the other cheek and put them to shame, except I don't believe they had any honour or shame. It was very apparent though, just how poor the country is, but if they treat their visitors like this, then is it any wonder. A bit later in the day, the police seemed to be a little friendlier towards me and I felt more at ease about leaving the boat. I went for a very long walk and stopped at the pizza shop on the way back. I was becoming a regular in there and knew the owner by name, "Good afternoon Hassem" I said. He knew exactly what I was going to ask for and prepared me an excellent pizza, as always. More recently he had started putting a few chips in the corner of the takeaway box for me. As the evening drew in, I sat at my outside table, enjoying my meal. Towing my boat away, I was thinking, they can't even tie theirs up, then I thought how sick I would be if they used the line I had spliced to do it. There was still an open bottle of wine in the fridge, I enjoyed what was left and took myself to bed.

I slept better that night and woke feeling quite refreshed, even the ribs were a lot less painful after four weeks of taking things easy. It looked like being a hot day, so I decided to finish the sunshade and put it up. Once done, it was very homely on the afterdeck and what's more the police couldn't see me. Before, I'd felt like a goldfish in a bowl. Well tomorrow was judgment day, at last I will know just how painful this is all going to be. I sat up until the small hours, there was no point in going to bed, I wouldn't be able to sleep. My head was spinning and there was nothing I could do to take my mind off things. I didn't know if I would hear in the morning or the afternoon. I checked my phone battery; it needed a charge so I plugged it in. Eventually, I went to bed and managed a couple of hours sleep. A motor scooter woke me as a policeman arrived for work at 6:30 am. No tea or breakfast, I picked up my phone and went for a brisk walk, this was going to be a very long day. At last, my phone rang at 11:45 am, I composed myself and answered, yes good morning what's the news then. The lawyer told me that the judgment had been postponed for fourteen days. "But why?" I asked "Whatever for?" "Well," he said "the Judge has asked Customs to produce all the paperwork including the form that you signed when you arrived." "Well hasn't he already seen it? I mean what's the point of a hearing if he hasn't got the document that all my charges rest on?" Customs didn't produce it." he said. "There's nothing we can do except wait."

I was furious, if Grey Suit and Smiles were here now, I swear, I would have killed the pair of them, and Slithering Sid as well for that matter. The thought of waiting around for another two weeks to hear my fate, sent my morale to rock bottom. The news had obviously got back to the police; they were sneering at me from the balcony and seemed seriously pissed off that I had managed to slip through the net again. Their behaviour turned quite aggressive, they were trying to intimidate me.

CHAPTER 6

The Intimidation

I was moored just five metres away from the Police building and the six metre high balcony ran the whole length of the frontage. At the end, on the right hand side and slightly set back, was an observation tower around fourteen metres high with Radar on the flat roof. Further inside the harbour and in clear view, there was a National Guard base housing 4 or 5 fast launches. I couldn't so much as clean my teeth, without them knowing about it. The previous night I had heard the side of the boat rubbing against the concrete wall, I went up to move the fenders around at just after 2 am and instantly there was a call from the balcony, "yes Captain what are you doing?" I rubbed the palms of my hands together in a chafing motion and went below without speaking at all. The next evening just after dark but with still some background noise about the place, I started the main engine. Within seconds there were three goons on the balcony, "Just charging my batteries" I said and went inside. It was almost impossible to get the boat out of here and to try, would only add to my list of charges and worsen the whole situation. I found myself slipping into survival mode and started to make my contingency plans.

Over the last month, I had developed a severe dislike towards this bunch of muppets and crazy things were going through my mind. Onboard I had enough normal household cleaning products, some sugar and other energy agents that would make a right mess of their poorly constructed building. I even had a plastic bucket and a wooden handled boat hook to mix it with. Anyone who knows about these things will tell you, it's not the making or placing of the device, the trick is to blow it from a safe distance away. During the search they had taken an air rifle that a child could own and left me with the flare pistol and all the cartridges that would do the job nicely.

Of course I wasn't seriously considering actually doing it but it brought a smile to my face. Anyway, I don't think my fellow countrymen would have been very amused by one of their own, blowing up Government buildings in a Muslim country during peace time. Laughing to myself, I turned my thoughts to more plausible options.

On my previous walks I had mentally mapped the town out pretty well, I knew the train station and bus stops, the taxi ranks and car hire offices. But anyway, I could walk out of here, carrying my back pack with my most treasured personal effects in. I could head north and commandeer a small yacht in the night, to sail across to Sicily, or would probably get away with boarding the ferry as a foot passenger. There were small fishing boats all around me that were coming in and out around the clock. They were usually rowed by two men, were wooden in construction, low in the water and most of them, dark blue in colour. I would have been virtually invisible on the radar and to the patrol boats at night. If I waited for a light breeze from the south, I could roll the sunshade up with some pieces of light line inside and use the oars to put up a makeshift jury rig, once I was at sea. I went to

the chart table to measure the distance, I noticed that there was a one knot current running from north to south, along the coast. If the wind failed me, I couldn't row a two man boat far against that, alone and anyway, my ribs still weren't a hundred percent. To end up in Libya, would be jumping out of the frying pan into the fire. That was a complete no brainer.

I still didn't know for sure if they were going to take my boat and I wasn't about to abandon it, until it happened. Getting myself out would only be to evade a custodial sentence. If it was down to paying a fine that I could afford, then I would just sail away with a bitter taste in my mouth. If I couldn't pay the fine then I was sure they would snatch the boat. This was my home and all my worldly goods were on board it, with my power tools, clothes, my kitchen ware, and crockery, everything. If it came down to it, I would buy an old van and load as much as I could into it, then drive it all home. When I had finished with it, I could sell it to a scrap dealer and probably get half my money back and would have salvaged my belongings. Of course, there would be nothing clandestine about it, loading the van right outside the Police station but I would be free to leave then or I hoped I would.

The thought of seeing my boat for the last time in the rear view mirror of a van was deeply depressing; this was very different to losing one of Her Majesty's Land Rovers in the middle of a desert somewhere. I found a piece of paper and began making a check list, I should definitely include engine oil, distilled water, jump leads, toolbox and anything else I may need on the overland trip. When finished, I set about packing my backpack. It would be ready if I needed it and if not, it could come with me in the van.

I couldn't think of any other preparations to make, except to prepare myself for whatever was coming. I went to sit outside in the breeze and take stock of things. There was a guard on the tower, holding what looked like a famos infantry assault rifle, casually pointing in my general direction. It had a magazine attached, so by definition, it was a loaded weapon. Of course, I had no way of knowing if the magazine contained any ammunition or not, but that wasn't the point, he was well out of order. But then they all were, the whole boat was covered in cigarette ends and ash that the goons on the balcony had very accurately disposed of, whenever I wasn't looking. They were also making a present of their orange peel and date stones among other things, this was seriously annoying, but what could I do.

I was having trouble dealing with this. In a conflict, one could return the aggression and was invariably with well trusted friends and colleagues; I was sat here alone, powerless to do anything. As the weather got progressively warmer, the goons started to remove their jackets, I was able to make a mental note of which ones were armed. One of them particularly amused me; he was wearing jeans and trainers with a kind of sports top and was carrying a side arm on his belt. The holster was loose on his belt and made of very supple leather, which allowed the pistol to hang at its point of balance with the barrel pointing slightly back. Ammunition is heavy and my bet was that the magazine he had in the pistol grip contained nothing. But he was strutting around like a very important little man. If he were to do that anywhere in Europe, he would have probably been shot by an armed rapid response unit. Of course, I would have mourned for several seconds.

The goons would arrive for work early in the morning and make a point of having a loud conversation right beside the boat, and late at night more of the same. They were doing everything possible, in a subtle way, to devil me into doing something rash. The next morning I took my cup of tea and sat at the outside table, there was a slimy green mess on top of the sunshade with a trace of tobacco stain, no bird had done that, the vermin were spitting on me now. It had been many years since I lost my temper but I was getting very close to it now. The wind had changed direction in the night and was now blowing directly onto the building. Breakfast time I think, I opened a tin of bacon grill and put the frying pan on the gas, then opened all the hatches, now it's my turn. I cooked it for far longer than necessary and wafted as much bacon smell out as I could.

Two days later I awoke to find a cigarette burn on the sunshade. That was the end of my patience. I went below and found a transparent plastic bag, then collected the cigarette ends and other rubbish from on deck. I took the bag to the door; the outer door was iron railings and latched back. The inner door was glass and I could see someone sitting behind the desk, I had one hand free but I didn't use it, I kicked the door twice, quite firmly, with my foot. When he opened the door, I thought he was about to wet himself. I tossed the open bag to him at chest height. He fumbled trying to catch it, as he did, I said "Now you can add returning lost property to my list of charges." I have no idea what my face must have looked like, but he couldn't close the door quick enough. I didn't see much more of them at all that day.

CHAPTER 7

Judgment postponed again

The following day the goons slowly started to emerge more and more, their attitude seemed to have changed for the better, but they were still very standoffish and very cold. I really don't think they quite knew what I would do next. They were still eating their oranges on the balcony like a load of Baboons on a rock, but none of the peel came in my direction. We seemed to have arrived at a stalemate and I was in no mood to give any ground at all.

Each day, they flexed their muscles a little more, but didn't actually cross the line. But I did, there was a blind spot on the left side of the building. Once past the door and the window, I couldn't be seen at all. Two metal posts were buried in the concrete and a chain lay on the ground. It could be clipped to the post near the building to prevent vehicular access whenever required.

I went for my pizza a bit late that evening and returned after dark. I clipped the chain in place. If they were going to arrive on their motor scooters and make as much noise as they possibly could, then I would at least wake up laughing tomorrow. The inevitable happened and in seconds, I was peering out through the wheelhouse windows, there was a scooter on the ground and a goon hopping beside it. As they were arguing about which idiot had secured the chain, I split my sides with laughing. One of them looked in my direction and said something, then they all looked. It was obvious that they suspected me but proving it would be a bit difficult. After that, the degradation and intimidation stopped completely, they now knew that their tactics weren't working and that I could be equally as nasty as they could.

On the voyage in, my poor ship's flag had received a real flogging during the storm and was looking in a bit of a sorry state. When I arrived, their national flag on top of the building was in a worse state than mine and was left flying over night. Although the courtesy flag was new, I purposely left mine, as it was and followed suit, so as not to appear arrogant. But now, I found the biggest and newest replacement that I had and hoisted it with pride, I also made a big thing about lowering it every night. We were engaged in our own private little cold war and outnumbered as I was, they were not exactly winning hands down.

My biggest concern now, was leaving the boat unattended, just as they couldn't prove the chain prank, if I returned to find any damage it would be touché. We were now in the later part of April and there was a tourist's day trip boat on the quay in front of me. Quite a large boat and left no room for visiting yachts to berth. Any incoming boats were being moored alongside me; this meant, of course, that I had police and customs clambering over the boat to get to them and the visitors doing the same to get ashore.

On the positive side, while they were onboard next to me, I was able to leave the boat and pick up a few supplies without worrying. What was a worry, would be leaving the boat to visit the court on judgment day. The date and time would be dictated to me and the goons would no doubt know this well before I did. I sat there racking my brains; I could be away for half the day at least. An idea came to me; Hassem in the pizza shop spoke some English and was one of the few trusted friends that I had managed to make here. At the next opportunity, I said "Hassem, my boat is beginning to get very dirty, I need a cleaner do you know anyone?" Being his normal, helpful and friendly self, he said "Yes, I have two friends who do this" and he picked the phone up. By the time my pizza came out of the oven, it was all organised. He told me what their services would cost and a flexible arrangement was in place. I explained that I was a bit busy just at the moment and enquired as to how much prior notice his friends needed. "Call me the day before" he said and wrote his number on my takeaway box. Well I could stop worrying about that now.

The days passed slowly and the standoff with the goons continued, visiting boats came and left from time to time, which allowed me a bit of exercise ashore. It was now the 23rd of April and judgment day was looming up again. After what seemed like a decade, I found myself sitting outside on the afternoon of the 27th feeling rather nervous again. Tomorrow it could all be over, then my phone rang. The lawyer told me that the judges were on strike and there would be no judgment tomorrow. "Well, how long for?" I asked. "Only two days" he said, "but there will be a backlog of work to clear so we can expect to hear in a week or so. This is good for us because the courts still haven't received the documents from the customs and if they arrive in the mean time it will prevent another postponement."

I was now convinced that customs were using every trick in the book to wait for the judge's decision. If he found me guilty, there was no telling what they would fine me. But the court was not in a hurry to make a rash decision, which had to be a good thing.

A couple of days later I called the lawyer," Look," I said "I know there is a delay with the court but what about the issue with customs have you any news on that?" He told me that the head of customs and his five immediate underlings had just been removed from office because of corruption; the newly appointed man hadn't been signed in yet. He told me as soon as the changeover was done he intended to arrange a meeting with the new man. After the call my spirits lifted considerable, so where were we now?

During my detainment in this dreadful place I had met several other visiting boats and all but one of them had a complaint of some sort about customs. Mainly breakages, due to heavy handed searching or dismantling things until the crew produced a bottle of whisky. One boat with a young couple and their child onboard told me about their arrival in Monastir, further up the coast. At 3 am they had dragged the poor child from her bed and she stood there terrified and whimpering as customs ransacked her bed. The father grabbed two bottles of wine and said "now leave."

The Tunisian government were obviously aware that there were big problems and to their credit had dealt with it severely. I couldn't help wondering if Grey Suit and Smiles were among the six, and I certainly hoped they were.

Head of customs was a very respected and influential position, in this part of the world and I was sure that the newly appointed man would want to make a good impression. Also, he would be aware that the appropriate minister would be watching him carefully, initially anyway. The timing was perfect; if the lawyer put my story across, he would have to be seen to act correctly. I was now feeling a lot better and just a little cocky too, the devilment started to get the better of me. It was time to play a few mind games with the Baboons on the rock.

I took my iPad on deck and sat at the table. I began to pretend to type, it wasn't even turned on but they couldn't see that. With a look of concentration, I pretended to work away. It wasn't long before they became very curious and started strolling around in front of the office and getting closer and closer to the boat.

I pretended not to notice them at all, indeed I was in deep concentration. After a while, I heard a voice and looked up with a surprised face. "What you do with your time?" "Oh, I'm writing another letter to one of your government ministers" I said. "Another?" he said "You write before." "Erm," I said and nodded my head with a very insincere smile on my face. "What you write?" he said. There were a few things that I felt he should know about I replied. He looked as though he had just been hit by a train; in no time at all they were back on their rock looking very sheepish. Without saying more than a few words, they were now under the impression that I may have been partly or even wholly responsible for the dismissal of the six men.

Over night their behaviour changed incredibly, our little cold war seemed to have ended, and I wasn't about to keep it going. They had now found some new manners and even some respect, all superficial of course. That didn't matter to me at all, just as long as they were off my back at last, and anyway I could be just as superficial as they could. They obviously valued their jobs and all wanted to be my best friend now. I adjusted my attitude, according to their individual approaches. It certainly seemed safe to leave the boat unattended, after all, it was directly in front of a police station.

I waited for another two days and decided to play my joker. The next morning, I dressed wearing grey flannel trousers, white shirt and tie and carrying my blazer over my arm. I politely tapped on the door, "Good morning" I said, "look I have to attend a meeting in Tunis today, would you keep an eye on my boat please?" One of them said "a meeting? Why?" I said "Sorry but I'm going to miss the train" and hurried away. I had a wonderful day away from it all, lunch in a fine hotel and a pleasant afternoon sight seeing and relaxing. They, on the other hand, were now the worried ones.

When I returned, the boat was just as I had left it, the outer railings door of the office was locked and they were all inside, I was pleased about that, I wasn't in the mood to be quizzed.

The next morning I received a text message from the lawyer which was unusual, he would normally call. When I read the message I understood why he had avoided the call. He couldn't bring himself to tell me that the judgment had been postponed again, this time until the 2nd of June.

CHAPTER 8

Hearts & Minds

That took a bit of swallowing, and meant another four weeks stuck here, but the situation had improved considerably. It suddenly occurred to me that the judge would almost certainly know about the customs' changes of personnel, and why. I couldn't help wondering if he was stalling, to see that no injustice was done. Anyway, I had to stay here until the 2nd of June at least, and maybe even longer. The police were now behaving very correctly, so I will stop referring to them as goons and baboons. But having knocked them over, I now would try and win them over. I decided to launch my own little Hearts & Minds campaign.

A few days before, a fisherman whose boat was tied up around the corner and just feet away from my stern, had introduced himself in quite good English, his name was Ali. He and his crew mates would arrive, usually around late afternoon or early evening loaded down with fish.

This particular day they moored up looking as though they had all had a long hard day, they certainly landed a lot of fish. I had just opened my takeaway box and had eaten only one slice of the pizza. I watched as they loaded their fine catch into a van. Their day wasn't over yet, their gear had fouled something and the nets were in need of repair before the morning. They were now sitting on the quay, mending their nets and the police were on the balcony having just watched all the fish being loaded up. They were quite surprised when I called Ali by his name. "Ali," I said "I can't eat this, it's very spicy. It's blowing my head off" and passed him the rest of the pizza. Actually, I love hot food and I'm a real curry freak. They were obviously hungry and put the net repairs on hold, while they enjoyed my offering.

The following evening I returned to find a very nice fresh fish in a carrier bag and carefully placed in the shade. I noticed their stern line was chafing on the concrete and there was wind forecasted for during the night. I spent a few minutes, splicing it for them. Before I made the splice, I threaded the line through a short length of flexible plastic hosepipe, it was now as strong as new, and protected from further chafing. I was still in bed when they put to sea, early the next morning. On their return, Ali was holding the repaired line up and pointing to my splice, "This was you" he said; "Yes, it was windy in the night." I replied. "Thank you my friend, thank you very much." he said, and began passing me more fresh fish.

This time, I lit the gas barbecue and in no time at all, I was passing delicious pieces of freshly cooked fish back, wrapped in tin foil. A policeman was on the quay; I beckoned him over and passed him a piece too.

Within a few days I had almost half the fishermen in the port onside, when passing they would pause for a handshake and we would communicate the best that we could, by making hand gestures. What a transformation, in less than a week, I had risen from despised criminal to quite a popular guy.

The next day one of the policemen was pushing his scooter up and down trying to start it. I could smell the petrol from onboard the boat, it was obviously flooded. I delved into my toolbox and went to him with a sparkplug spanner. A few minutes later, he was riding it away with a big grin on his face. I didn't know it at the time, but his father was a police chief in another district. I had noticed before, that he seemed to be respected among his colleagues and considering his young age and low rank, I had wondered why. There was now no problem at all with leaving the boat unattended, I went walking and shopping whenever the mood took me, I was now getting more exercise than a Greyhound trainer.

Over the last few weeks when I believed there was a real chance of losing my boat, I just couldn't muster the enthusiasm to do any cleaning. Having made an arrangement with Hassem I didn't want to let him down or waste his time, the boat needed a clean anyway, so I called him. The next morning, two absolutely gorgeous young ladies turned up at the boat, ready for work. Some of the younger policemen were very soon strutting about on the quay, desperately trying to be noticed. The girls had already started work inside. I said "Look, it's going to get hot later, would you like to clean outside first and work inside later in the shade?" They thought that was a good plan and went on deck. The young lads wasted no time at all in bidding them good morning and striking up a conversation, and of course the girls were loving all the attention.

There was a rat trap under the office window beside the door and over night, a rat had entered the cage. One of the youngsters started patting the top of the cage firmly with his hand. As the rat reacted they all laughed and his friends began to egg him on, for a few minutes it was a right circus act. The police were now so close to the side of the boat that they were almost helping to polish it with their jackets. The fact that the girls were being paid by the hour and weren't exactly doing very much didn't bother me at all. I was now almost as holy as the guy who hung out of the Mosque tower singing for all he was worth at 4:30 am every morning.

Just then, two National Guard men rounded the corner and decided this area needed patrolling for a while and were now competing with the others for the girls' attention. One of them was carrying a rifle, slung on his shoulder, with the muzzle pointing downwards, in a safe direction. He decided to muscle in, by chatting to the girls' employer, me. I stepped ashore and greeted him, then pretended to admire his assault rifle. I flicked the magazine twice, with my forefinger in quick succession. The sound told me it was full, or very nearly, anyway. "It's French?" I asked. "Yes," he said "Famos carbine, very good." It wasn't many days ago that he had been pointing it at me from his tower; well at least his safety catch was applied. No need to dwell on that I thought, especially if they were now onside as well. As the day got hotter, the girls started work inside, and they did work too, they left me with a very clean boat that afternoon and had done wonders for my integration effort.

The Hearts & Minds approach had been a complete success and the rest of my unwanted stay here was going to be a lot easier than the past weeks. I knew that I mustn't let things slip and continued to integrate, in any way possible. A day or two later a young boy of maybe ten years old, wheeled his bicycle past the boat, he was holding the back wheel clear off the ground, by the seat and looking as though he was having a bad day. The chain had come off and jammed itself behind the sprocket, so that the wheel would no longer turn. He had grazed one knee quite badly and was limping slightly; I grabbed a large screwdriver and went to his rescue. It only took seconds to prize the jammed chain free, but during this time, his eyes were all over the boat, I think he was asking to come and have a look. I didn't think it was appropriate to be inviting children onboard, alone and anyway, he was a dirty little tyke and I had a clean boat now. I gave him a pat on the back and said "Get out of here." A policeman on the balcony had seen it all, he gave me what appeared to be a very genuine smile and nodded his head slowly as if to demonstrate his approval. I had achieved my goal; all I had to do now was sit it out.

CHAPTER 9

The Conclusion

There were now 17 days left to wait for my next court appearance and hopefully there would be a fair judgment that would end all of this mess, as painlessly as possible. On the morning of the 17th, one of the policemen tapped on the side of the boat, "Customs have asked for you, they want you to go to their office." "What for?" I asked. "They didn't say, you must just go." he replied.

I instantly thought that the newly appointed man, must have signed my papers and that would be part of the problem solved anyway. As long as I could afford the fine, I'd get my boat back and have freedom of movement again.

I changed my clothes and made my way into town, wondering as I walked, how the day would unfold. It wasn't far, I would know soon enough, but my pace quickened anyway. I had been waiting weeks to resolve this and the anxiety was getting the better of me.

The building was familiar to me from my previous visits in March and I knew exactly which office to go to. When I tapped on the door and wished them good morning, I was surprised to see the same translator already waiting for me. I was told to sit in the usual place and a document was placed on the table, in Arabic, of course.

"This is your reconciliation with customs." the translator told me and began to translate it to me. "Look, take your time," I said "we don't want any more nasty little surprises later do we?" He knew I was referring to his previous conduct, but didn't show any embarrassment or shame at all. When he was finished, I said "So I have to pay 2900 Dinars? I thought you said we could negotiate this." "Customs won't negotiate," he said, "talk to your Lawyer." "Never mind" I said and produced my bank card.

"No, not this, dinars only dinars." "But you called me about an hour ago, I don't carry that much money around with me." "You have ninety days to pay, but only dinars, come when you have the money." That was fine by me, because I could send the document by email to my lawyer, before I paid, to double check things.

Later, on the boat, I photographed the document and emailed him asking why he hadn't been able to reduce the fine, it was actually 100 dinars more. In the late afternoon, he replied saying that customs just put his calls on hold and basically refused to cooperate, but the document was good. If I paid, the papers would be returned and the boat was mine again. I resigned myself to the fact that before the recent personnel changes, I had absolutely no way of knowing what the fine would eventually be. At least the new man had signed the original valuation of the guns 2800 dinars and only added 100 dinars.

It would have taken me a week to draw that amount, if I visited the cash point machine every day and drew the maximum. I had spotted a bank with a Weston Union sign outside, not far from the boat. It was time to email my poor brother and ask for yet another little favour. The sooner I had my papers back, the better. By 11 am the next morning, the money was in my pocket and on its way to the customs office.

They seemed quite surprised to see me so soon, after a few minutes they had amassed all their paperwork and I was escorted to the payment kiosk. There was another man just paying a 30 dinar fine and looking very upset about it, his jaw dropped to the floor when he saw me hand over my huge wad of 100 dinar notes, he left shaking his head. I was given a receipt for the money and they began preparing another document. Then, to add insult to injury, they demanded a further 3 dinars to put their stamp on it. We went back to the office to finalise everything and the document was taken away to be signed by their boss.

I was sat in the prisoners chair again and they went about their normal business completely ignoring me. I waited and waited, watching the clock on the wall, after forty five minutes I asked if there was a problem of some kind. "No problem" they said, "you must wait." So I continued to sit there. After another half an hour, I asked again and was told the boss wasn't in his office. Well he was, because I could hear him talking and his car was parked outside.

I knew them all by now and their cars. Even at this late stage, they were intent on being the biggest arsholes that they could possibly be. They made me wait all afternoon, until just before closing time and as soon as the translator arrived, so did the document. The rest didn't take very long, just one more dodgy translation, then they handed me the boat registration papers and two photocopies. One was a copy of my receipt and one was a copy of my firearms license. "What's this?" I said "I want the originals." "It's the same" they said. "No it is not the same, the originals are mine and I want them back now as per the reconciliation document yesterday, I've paid the fine in full now, you must return everything."

Reluctantly they gave me the originals and the new document with my nice 3 Dinar stamp on it. I couldn't quite understand why they wanted to keep the originals, the court case was looming up again it could only be something to do with that. But the lawyer had told me that, although customs had filed the charges against me, the court was a completely separate issue.

I took a Taxi back to the boat, so as to forward my new document to the lawyer before it got too late. When I arrived, the police were hovering around the boat and instantly started to quiz me. I produced my papers and said "Yes everything is okay now." "So, you are a free man" they said. "Yes I am." I replied, but I didn't remind them of the pending court case.

Back onboard, I photographed and forwarded to the lawyer again. It was nearly 6pm now and I didn't expect to hear from him, but it would be in his inbox first thing in the morning. It still hadn't really sunk in that I was a free man. I could go out for a sail or even move to a nicer port, what a lovely feeling that was. I put some pasta on the hob and decided the occasion called for a little celebration, I uncorked a nice bottle of red wine and began to chill out, heaven knows I needed it, I was going to sleep a lot easier tonight.

At 9 am the next morning the lawyer called, "This document is not correct." he told me, "They have not mentioned the air rifle, it says two shotguns and your firearms certificate is for one shotgun, this will cause problems in court, you must go back and get it changed.

Well it was now plainly obvious why they wanted to keep the originals and that slimy translator had shafted me, again. I took a few seconds to get a grip of my temper then said, "I'm not going back, not alone anyway, it's absolutely pointless, they will just have me over again. I have all my papers back and if they go to court with falsified evidence, then you should bring this to the judge's attention and also it's about time you mentioned that the translator is a lying snake." He said "I understand your frustration, but at least you have your freedom back, I'll call you if there is any news." Later, he sent me a text message asking me again to try and correct the document, I didn't reply.

This was completely crazy, even though the charges were totally false I was doing my very best to go along with the legal system and comply in every respect. But comply with what, there was no justice here, they moved the goal posts and changed the rules whenever they felt like it, it was impossible to achieve a just outcome. There was no chance of recuperating any of the money that I had already lost and even if the judge ruled in my favour, I still had to pay the berthing fees. And there could be another adjournment, so if he fined me or not, I would still be paying the lawyer and the berthing fees. This was a total no win situation. In the late afternoon, he called again to ask if I had corrected the document, and took the opportunity to mention his fees. He told me that he would have to drive down from Tunis again, on the afternoon of the 1st to accompany me in court early on the 2nd, he would need another 1000 Dinars but when I paid before, by bank transfer it had cost him 45 Dinars in bank charges, so could I give him the cash, when he met me at the court.

I was becoming very fed up with being milked dry by everyone here and he had achieved nothing, the customs had run rings round him for the last ten weeks and we were still nowhere with the court.

To date, I had lost just over 9000 Dinars in confiscated goods, fines, berthing costs, translator fees and legal costs. The berthing costs were a joke; the place could only be described as a serious health hazard. There was raw sewage overflowing from the police station manhole, just feet away and constantly running down the harbour wall, right beside the boat. The rats were competing with the seagulls for the rotten fish that was laying around in the sun and the stench was nauseating. Fishermen were urinating all over the quay and sleeping on the piles of net that also stunk. The whole place was heavily littered with rubbish and the water was permanently covered in an oil slick. I had been forced to endure this, since I arrived on the 16th of March and I had had enough.

Since my arrival, I had been ripped off, short changed and cheated by every market stall, shopkeeper and street trader that I had purchased from, with the exception of my friend in the pizza shop.

It is true to say that out of necessity I spent most of my time onboard the boat for security reasons. That's another joke, just five metres away from a police station, but it meant that I hadn't socialised much, at all, and so had met very few local people, other than on a business footing. Having said that, in the nearly ten years that I had lived on my boat and travelled around visiting many countries, never before had I felt the need to secure the boat and lock myself in at night, but here I did every night.

If one were to visit a tourist destination on a package holiday, it is likely that you would enjoy your stay with a group of other holiday makers, but outside of those areas the place is filthy and not particularly safe, in my mind anyway. I decided that my original plan to have the boat lifted out of the water here because of the cheap rates was no longer an option. Now that I had freedom of movement it would be a bit brain dead to immobilize it completely just to save a bit of money. In March, when two French boats were lifted out, here in Mahdia, the yard was a loose surface and uneven. This meant, that every time they pressure washed the underside of a boat, the water puddled in the low spots and they were working underneath their boats in a bog. Being French, they could communicate fluently, but when I walked round to the yard to make enquiries for my boat, they just couldn't be bothered with me.

I would pay a little more in a European port somewhere with concrete hard standing and shower facilities. Another reason for coming here was the low fuel prices; now that the boat was mine again, I should at least take advantage of that and fill up.

That evening I sat quietly and reflected on the situation, freedom of movement was a bit ambiguous, did that mean within Tunisian waters or total freedom to go where I like. I was not under arrest. Of course, we had no judgment yet, that was still a possibility. Why wait, just at their mercy, why not wash my hands of the whole unpleasant place and get the boat and myself back into Europe.

The courts had taken far too long to acquit an innocent man, and I couldn't count on that verdict anyway. I was now in a position to bring things to a conclusion myself. One thing was certain; I was absolutely sick and tired of being tucked up in Tunisia. I just wanted to get out of here.

CHAPTER 10

Getting out

So that was it then I wasn't going to wait around or be messed around any more, these people were making a complete fool of me and robbing me every step of the way, but I needed to do this very carefully.

Time was on my side now, the berth was paid for another week, I had internet access and could monitor the weather carefully and could take on fuel just two hundred metres away, on the other side of the harbour. Tonight I would think things through and forge a plan, tomorrow I would take fuel onboard. I mustn't do anything quickly or give them any cause for suspicion; it must all be very casual. Even after I had paid the fine, they were still trying to stitch me up in court, and their previous track record had demonstrated that they would stop at nothing to extort as much as they possibly could, whether it be right or wrong. If they caught me leaving without clearing through customs that would almost certainly be goodbye to my boat. Doing a runner without clearing through customs would be an absolute last resort, but if I sailed north, calling into various ports on the way, when I reached Kelibia I could steer for Sicily.

If I could pass the twelve mile limit and I would have done nothing wrong until I did, then I would be within VHF radio range of the Italian coastguard. If they tried to apprehend me in International waters, I could send a Mayday reporting an act of Piracy and they would hear this. If it came to that, I think they would return to Tunisian waters. An acceptable risk I thought, but only if all else failed.

One thing was for sure, they were never going to clear me out of the country from this port so I would have to find a reason to go to the next port along the coast which was Monastir.

The next morning I started the engine and began casting my mooring lines off. Instantly a policeman said "Where are you going? You need a form from us to take to your next port." "I'm only going to buy some fuel and I'm coming straight back, I've been charging my batteries with the engine for ten weeks, I'm very low on fuel." "Okay" he said. "My berth is paid for until the end of the week" I said, "surely you're not going to kick me out after all this time, I'm part of the furniture now." He smiled and disappeared inside but they were obviously still watching me like a Hawk. I moored up, alongside the diesel pump and waited for the pump attendant, Jack had warned me to watch the metre carefully, because the chap is prone to winding the metre on, when you're not looking. "How much do you want?" he said. "I think around 700 ltr" I replied, "but I have two tanks and it's difficult to know exactly." I made sure the metre was at zero and started pumping. From the filler cap on this side, I could see everything. When this tank was nearly full, I called to him and he walked towards me which allowed me to read the metre, then I changed to the other side tank. As I began filling, he was pretending to not understand, he held up six fingers and said "seven hundred." I said "No that's six" and held up seven fingers. "I'll stop when it's full." The wheelhouse was between me and the pump, so I was leaving the nozzle for a few seconds to watch the metre. I read 540 litres and in the time it took me to return to the nozzle, he had stopped the pump. When I turned round, he was holding up six fingers again and saying seven. The pump was now reading 600 litres, which meant it had delivered 60 litres in around four seconds. The thieving swine had caught me; I said "this is not right, you have tampered with the metre." He pretended to be angry that I would suggest such a thing, so I became angry also, "I need another 100 litres and you get yourself away from the pump or you'll be going for a swim," he understood that quite well.

Later in the office, I said that's 650 litres then, 700 he said. "I'm paying for the 650 litres that I had and no more." "You pay or I call the police" he said. What do I do now, I thought. I know what I'd like to do, but this was no time to be getting into more trouble, it was just one more robbery in a long line of robberies, I would be out of here soon enough. The really annoying thing was that taking into account the fuel I had used to get here and the thief on the pump, I hadn't saved anything at all. I went back to my berth and tied up, then started measuring distances on the chart. That was the final straw, I was well ready to leave this hell hole now.

So now I had full tanks and all my documents onboard, things were looking better, but what was this form I needed from the police. I would ask casually later, when the opportunity arose. Later two policemen were chatting on the quay, I put some water in a bucket and started to mop the afterdeck, "There's a lot of dust in the wind," I said "it's getting everywhere." "That's normal here." they said, "It comes from the desert." "Look" I said "I have some friends sailing into Monastir later in the week, I want to sail up there and join them for a few days, what's this piece of paper you mentioned this morning?" "You must tell us before you leave and we will prepare it for you to produce at your next port." "Okay thanks" I said, "that's likely to be Friday morning." "Yes, no problem" they answered, "but what about the court? Are you coming back?" Oh blast they were suspicious I needed to think quickly and answer this one right. "Not with the boat" I said, "my lawyer is driving down from Tunis, to attend court with me, so he will pick me up on his way down." They seemed quite satisfied with that and I went back to my cleaning. If they were going to let me leave here, I had a reasonable chance of clearing out through any one of several ports along the coast and there was still a week before the court case. I wouldn't be in any more trouble until, I failed to appear in court and by then I should be safely away.

The weather forecast was the all important thing now, I must keep a close eye on that and between now and my departure I could shop for biscuits, chocolate and other convenient high energy food. The night before, I would cook up a pot of stew and grab some fresh bread. I was beginning to feel confident but very run down, over the last ten weeks, I had been subjected to untold amounts of stress and it had taken it's toll. My joints ached, my head was dull and I had lost weight, rest was what I needed now.

As the week slowly passed, I went for walks and gradually collected my ship's stores. As much as I tried, I couldn't relax, I was wound up tighter than a drum skin.

The day before I looked at the weather, Monastir was only thirty sea miles away, taking into account the dangerous shoals that I would have to skirt round. It was all looking good, I would leave here in the morning and arrive in Monastir in the afternoon, looking like a regular tourist. The next morning I was up and about very early. By the time the police started to arrive, I had shaved and had a good breakfast. I reminded them that I was leaving and asked if they could prepare my paperwork, they did so and by 8.30 am I was clear of the harbour entrance and on my course. Progress was slow because of the barnacles and mussel farm that I had acquired below the waterline. But step one had worked, I was out of Mahdia and heading north. I turned the radar on, even though the visibility was very good, just to see if I was being tailed, there were some boats about but no one seemed to be following my course. I made the best speed I could with motor and sail constantly keeping a close eye on the radar. Around midday I nearly ran into an unmarked fishing net, I spotted it just in time and put the engine full astern, it was probably 600 metres long and only visible by the floats on the surface, no flags or marks at all. Because I had the sail up, it was a bit of a panic being singlehanded and delayed me by half an hour or so, but I was scheduled to arrive in good time with plenty of daylight to spare, the rest of the trip was pretty uneventful.

As I approached the harbour entrance, I called the marina office to arrange a berth and asked for some help to moor up, the help was there when I arrived and I was put alongside a concrete wall in front of some restaurants, quite an improvement.

In fact, it was a nice marina, clean and with good facilities. The water wasn't particularly clean, I wouldn't want to swim in it or eat anything that came out of it, but it was a tourist resort and it suited me perfectly. I went to the office and paid for two nights. It was nice to be plugged into the shore power and have electricity again and a fresh water supply. I went for a nice long shower, then strolled around the marina, looking for a good place to eat tonight; it was treat myself time, I could put the washing machine on tomorrow and give the boat a hose down, tonight was mine.

I returned to the boat, having enjoyed a lovely meal for a very reasonable price and served by helpful and friendly waiters. What a totally different place this was. In the morning, I got busy with domestic chores and checked the engine over, ready for the next day. It suddenly dawned on me that I had quite a lot of Tunisian currency in my pocket and thought about how to spend it. I had been told about a nautical chandlery that was one kilometre away, so decided to buy a few things for the boat. Also, there was an exit tax to pay of 30 dinars, I called into the police office, on the way past and paid the money. They licked the stamp and stuck it in my passport, beside the entry stamp, so all I needed now was the custom's exit stamp inked over it. The chandlery had some useful things for a fair price, so I bought what I could carry and saved a little money to last until I was ready to leave. Walking back to the boat reminded me of Mahdia, it was heavily littered and a right mess.

I was pleased to get back into the marina complex. Back onboard, I put the kettle on and went online to check the weather. That was a nuisance, the forecast had changed completely. The wind direction had veered more northerly and was stronger than before. This meant I would be punching into the weather all the way and may have to put in a tack, which would increase the journey time. Anyway, regardless of the weather, I had to leave. If it meant setting a different course, then that's what I would do. It wasn't all bad, being a sailing boat, she is quite steady going into the wind, but if they did decide to give chase, it would be very bumpy in their motor launch. Also, the waves would clutter up their radar screen and make it harder to find me, and the weather could change again before tomorrow, so no need to fret just yet.

I planned to dine out again tonight, on the last of my money and was very much looking forward to it, then home for an early night. Tomorrow was the big day. I was feeling slightly more relaxed, in the more pleasant surroundings but wondered what would happen in the customs' office tomorrow. It took a long while to get off to sleep. Daylight woke me at 5.30 am and I jumped out of bed, like a man on a mission, and indeed I was. I walked to the showers and was back for the 6am weather update, which hadn't changed at all over night. I didn't want to leave too early, lunch in the port would be good and leave at 2 or 3 pm would be perfect. A few hours out and I would have the cover of darkness on my side, then by the morning it should all be over.

The morning passed very slowly, I tried to think of any other preparations that I may have overlooked, but there were none, I had even cleaned the instrument screens with a damp tissue paper. I was as ready as I could possibly be. It was nearly time to have an early lunch and a lay down. I dropped my shower key into the office and said goodbye, as I made my way to a steak restaurant that I had noticed yesterday. I was grinning to myself, because the money I had spent on the boat and myself, would otherwise have been spent on fines and costs.

After lunch, I managed an hour's sleep, then decided to try my luck in the customs' office. I was very nervous as I walked in and had no idea what to expect. I handed over my passport and was asked to sit at the desk. "You must collect your form from the police office next door and come back." they said. I did that and was seated again. "Your declaration, where is it?" "I don't have anything else, only this" I said. It suddenly hit me that the form I had signed when I arrived, thinking it was a port police form was now with the court at the judge's request, how on earth could I get round this one. I played the silly tourist and shrugged my shoulders, "That's all I have" I said. He looked at his colleague, rolled his eyes back and said "Mahdia huh." He made a short phone call, probably to his boss, then spun round on his chair and reached for a folder, he removed a blank form and placed it in front of me, "Complete this" he said. I couldn't believe my luck, they were clearing me out with no paperwork, it took no time at all for me to complete the form and as soon I was walking back to the boat, stamped and correctly cleared out of Tunisia.

I was a bit earlier than planned, but I wasn't going to wait around now. I started the engine and turned on the instruments, a security guard threw me the mooring lines and I was underway in minutes. Before 2 pm I was clear of the harbour. It was a bit rough but that didn't matter. All that mattered was the distance between me and the coast.

Very little was done here on a computer, it was all good old fashioned pieces of paper and rubber stamps. I had found the long delays and postponements, frustrating over the past weeks, but today it had worked in my favour. By the time they realised that they had screwed up big time, I would be miles away. The wind angle wasn't too bad and the course I was on was taking me more or less where I had planned. The radar wasn't showing any other ships, they all had more sense than to be out here today. Even the fishermen were giving me a clear run. Progress was slow but steady, we were crashing into the waves which were slowing the boat and there was still a mussel farm on the bottom of the poor old girl, but in just over an hour, we should be out of Tunisian waters. The radar screen was heavily cluttered, due to the sea state, but then I wasn't looking for them, they were looking for me. Except I didn't really believe that they were and if they were, they hadn't got long, because I was nearly out and had done it legally. What could they do until I fail to appear in court? I had done nothing wrong at all. We continued punching into the weather all through the night and by daybreak, the Italian island of Pantelleria was on the horizon. I was out and with the boat, what a huge relief. Of course, after failing to appear in court, I would be a wanted man in Tunisia and it would be unwise to visit again, but I cannot imagine ever wanting to. If I did, I would leave the boat somewhere safe and go across on the ferry with my backpack, and the purpose of my visit would be to rid the Tunisian population of eight very nasty men.

EIN HERZ FÜR AUTOREN A HEART FOR AUTHORS À L'ÉCOUTE DES AUTEURS MIA ΚΑΡΔΙΑ ΓΙΑ ΣΥΓΓΡΑ
HJÄRTA FÖR FÖRFATTARE UN CORAZÓN POR LOS AUTORES YAZARLARIMIZA GÖNÜL VERELIM SZÍV
CUORE PER AUTORI ET HJERTE FOR FORFATTERE EEN HART VOOR SCHRIJVERS TEMOS OS AUTOR
INFORMAÇÃO ВСЕЙ ДУШОЙ К АВТОРАМ A HEART FOR AUTHORS À L'ÉCOUTI
MIA ΚΑΡΔΙΑ ΓΙΑ ΣΥΓΓΡΑΦΕΙΣ UN CUORE PER AUTORI ET HJERTE FOR FORFATTERE EEN HA
YAZARLARIMIZA GÖNÜL SZÍVÜNKET ZOINKÉRT SERCE DLA AUTORÓW EIN HERZ FÜR
EEN HART VOOR SCHRIJVERS TEMOS OS AUTORES INFORMAÇÃO ВСЕЙ ДУШОЙ К АВТОРАМ ETT HJÄRTA FÖR

The author

The publisher

> Whoever stops
> getting better,
> will in time stop
> being good.

This is the motto of novum publishing, and our focus
is on finding new manuscripts, publishing them and
offering long-term support to the authors.
Our publishing house was founded in 1997, and since
then it has become THE expert for new authors and
has won numerous awards.

**Our editorial team will peruse each manuscript
within a few weeks free of charge and without
obligation.**

You will find more information about
novum publishing and our books on the internet:

www.novum-publishing.co.uk

Printed in Great Britain
by Amazon